FRANK SINATRA

A Life in Pictures **Edited by Yann-Brice Dherbier**

First published in Great Britain in 2011 by Pavilion
An imprint of Anova Books Company Ltd
10 Southcombe Street, London W14 0RA

© Anova Books Company Ltd

First published in France by YB Éditions
Biography © Frédéric Brun – 2011
Other text © YB Éditions – 2011
Front cover © MPTV / Sid Avery / Photomasi
Art Director: Renaud Sauteret (sauteret@mac.fr)
Translator: Alfred LeMaitre

A CIP catalogue record for this book is available from the British Library.

ISBN: 978-1-86205-925-2

Printed and bound in China

10 9 8 7 6 5 4 3 2 1

www.anovabooks.com

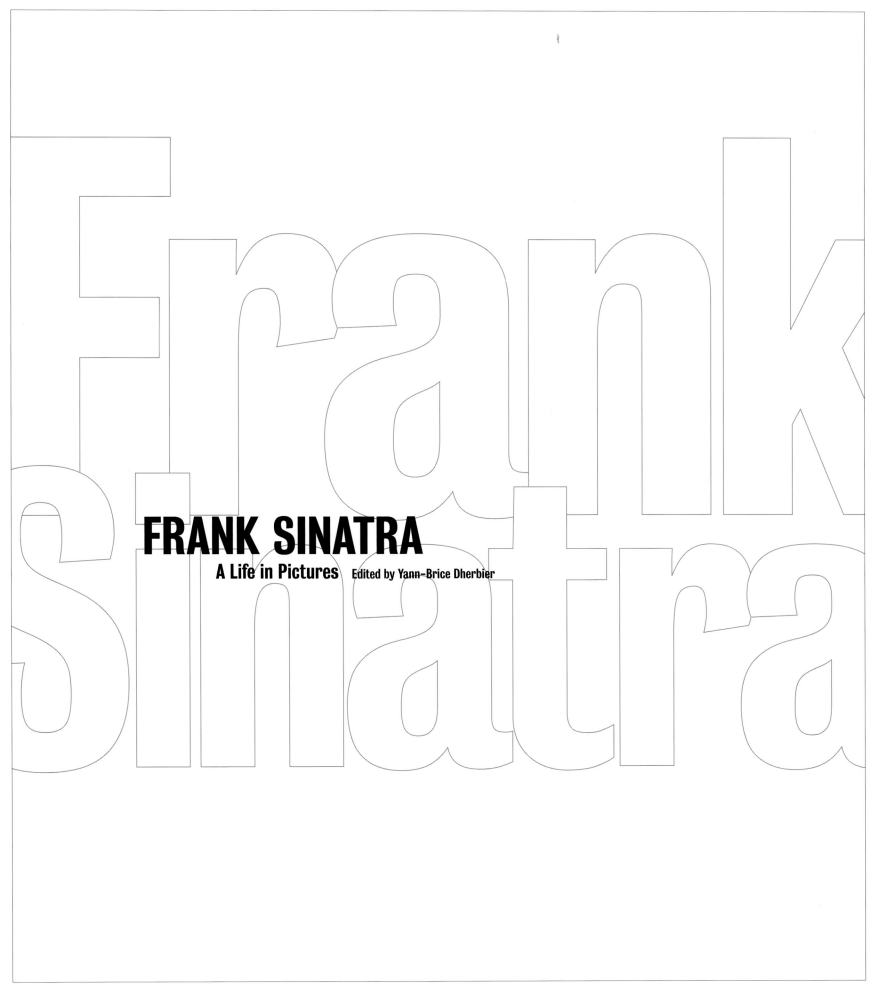

FRANK SINATRA

A Life in Pictures   Edited by Yann-Brice Dherbier

Frank Sinatra

FRANK SINATRA

The Chairman of the Board

Did all this really happen? During the last century, in an era where everything still seemed possible, there existed a man whose name was known on every continent and whose voice was familiar to millions of ears. He could soothe sadness and help bring back old memories. When he appeared in public, women fainted, men wanted to be his friend or copy his bow tie, and young girls were suddenly ready to depart this life. In the shadows, he made deals with thugs, made fun of morality and the law and associated with politicians. He had more money than anyone could ever spend, more success than anyone could imagine, more jets, more limousines, more villas, but he was never made an ambassador. He loved booze, gambling and his pack of friends. Nothing was impossible to him. He invented a style, started fashions, and sometimes forgot not to follow them for too long. He was excessively talented, excessively charming, excessively hated and excessively popular. His motto was 'all or nothing' – 'All or Nothing At All'. His voice was a magic spell; it was the soundtrack of lives that became, as if by magic, mega-productions in Cinemascope. All this happened during the 20th century, and it deserves to be told today. This is the story of a singer. Frank Sinatra.

'His name is Sinatra and he thinks he's the best voice in the business. Would you believe it? Nobody's ever heard him. He's never had a hit, and looks like a wet rag, but he says he's the greatest!' As she read in a local newspaper the words of bandleader Harry James, her son's musical partner, Mrs Sinatra could well have asked a few questions. Nevertheless, it was true that in 1939, Francis Albert Sinatra, a young man from Hoboken, New Jersey, started to make a name for himself. As his dreams took form, he set off on a journey of no return. The young Sinatra started out as a journalist for a small daily newspaper; he was always well-dressed in his Sunday suit, which he didn't like to get crumpled, even when he had the itch to start a fight or sort someone out. But when you're a fan of Bing Crosby, the idea of reporting local events for the *Jersey Observer* might feel narrow and constricting. Along with a number of other Hollywood stars, the velvet-voiced Crosby, so stylish and romantic, was the most admired man in America. In 1933, the young man saw Crosby perform live; the next day, Sinatra was strolling around in a tweed jacket, pipe in his mouth, even wearing a straw boater to ape his idol. Nothing would ever be the same again. He started singing everywhere he could, at the slightest opportunity, in the most obscure bar or club, wherever he could land a spot – generally as a waiter. From now on, everyone would know him simply as 'Frank'.

The diminutive form of his name went back a long way. His mother had called him Frank as a child, not out of an ability to simplify but because of politics. It was also the first name of Franklin Roosevelt, who became President in 1932. Natalie Sinatra was a strong woman, though everyone in Hoboken called her 'Dolly'. She was certainly strong, especially because she had an iron hand in a mailed fist. Her husband, Martin Sinatra, seemed puny next to her, even though she was only 1.5m (5ft) tall. A shoemaker from Lercara Friddi, outside Palermo, in Sicily, Martin became the local fire chief – thanks to Dolly's 'connections'. Charismatic and possessive, this Genoa-born mamma loved her son fiercely from the first, no doubt because his birth had been such a testing time.

The birth was very difficult, in fact. During the late afternoon of 12 December 1915, Dolly felt contractions and strong pain. Herself a midwife (and sometime abortionist), nicknamed 'the knitter' by the local union, she prepared for a painful labour. The baby presented badly, and the doctor who was hastily summoned that evening to 415 Monroe Street had to use forceps. While the doctor was attending to the mother, leaving what he thought was a stillbirth in a corner of the room, a cry suddenly arose. Rose Garaventi, Dolly's mother (and Frank's grandmother), had struck the infant, and passed him under cold water to make him react. The doctor's forceps had pierced an eardrum. Frank Sinatra would bear a scar as a result of his difficult birth, as well as partial deafness in the left ear, a condition he took no notice of until he decided to become a singer.

Dolly understood that this was getting serious one day in 1935, when she heard her son on the famous 'Major Bowes Amateur Hour', a popular radio show. Frank was getting on well with a trio called The Three Flashes. The producer decided to make them sing together, and the youngsters, unimaginatively renamed The Hoboken Four, won the competition. They started touring with the Major Bowes Travelling Show and picked up a few concert dates. Sinatra was hungry: he would do any radio show, pester bandleaders and sing in every club and bar he could – sometimes for next to no money, mostly for the fame. If he wanted to be noticed, he needed to acquire experience and benefit from maximum exposure.

Fame – that's what he wanted. With fame, all the rest – wealth, conquests – would come easily. Often short of money, but always a big spender with his friends, Sinatra was already a successful charmer. With young women, he was a born seducer. But sometimes he let himself fall into the 'tender trap' he later sang about. During the summer of 1935, while courting the young Nancy Barbato, he took her to a Bing Crosby concert. Things got more serious. Frank's mother was not opposed, even though her son had done it before.

On 26 November 1938, in between sets at the Rustic Cabin, a little bar where he sang – thanks to his mother's good relations with local politicians and unions – he was arrested. At the police station, he was photographed full-face and in profile with a small sign bearing the number 42799. The docket indicated that he was charged with 'seduction under the promise of marriage' to 'a single female of good repute for chastity'. Frank's reputation was made, even if he was released with a warning. One more time, his mother and his 'friends' were there. The case was dismissed. The merry-go-round started up again three or four times. Nancy Barbato threatened to break it off, but each time let herself be trapped by the charmer's pleading.

Little Nancy, Frank's teenage sweetheart, was also a Hoboken girl; Dolly liked the girl's Italian roots. On 4 February 1939, the couple were married. Following the ceremony, Frank presented his bride with a song he had recorded the night before: 'Our Love'. The young man established an Italian-style home, or so it seemed. She would certainly be the mother of his children, but the singer, intoxicated with his conquests, was very clear with her. One day when she complained about never being with him when he went to the Rustic Cabin, he declared brusquely: ' If I'm successful, I don't want to have to pull you along like a ball and chain.' Clearly, Frank himself was not the slightest bit burdened by moral principles when it came to conjugal matters.

A new arrest soon made a big splash in the local press. 'Nightingale in the cage for violating moral standards', crowed a local daily. Sinatra threatened the journalist. The escapade didn't matter; he was made like that. Towards the end of the 1960s, Sinatra had the nerve to tell journalists: 'I was giving back to those girls all the love they gave me. They wrote me thousands of letters, and every time I sang I made love to them.' Many times during his career, he proudly pinned a list of his future conquests to his dressing room door, circling each name in turn once the deed was done. But to call him a nightingale meant there would be blood on the floor. Throughout his career, his relations with the press were more like a boxing match.

Nancy was clearly affected. Frank was far from home on 8 June 1940, when their daughter Nancy was born, as he was in 1943 for the birth of their son Frank, Jr (only Tina, in 1948, would see the light of day under the eyes of her father). The singer owed much to his wife, who supported him in all his projects.

Hired as a waiter at the Rustic Cabin, and later as a backing singer, Frank decided to put his cards on the table and adopt a stage name. He had to be stylish and American: from that point he became Frankie Trent. He had already had to correct an error on his birth certificate (the registrar's clerk had misspelled his family name, officially baptizing him Frank Sinestra) ... a brochure at the entrance to the bar praised the 'leading man' Frankie Trent. Nancy disapproved of the name, and Dolly added her voice to the chorus. Mamma's anger was almost Homeric: 'There is no finer name, none more musical, than Sinatra!'

It was at this time that Frank attracted the attention of Harry James. The bandleader-arranger was putting together his great orchestra, a 'big band' of some thirty musicians. From the beginning, he unlocked Sinatra's talent, the magnetism of his voice, his implacable will, his fierce temper and his smouldering charm, his determination to get his name at the top of the bill as much as his boundless ego, his total bad faith and his arrogance. In only a few months, between 1939 and 1940, their partnership became one of the most creative of Sinatra's career. The singer recorded many songs at this time; on 31 August 1939, at Columbia Records studio, he recorded 'All or Nothing at All' with the Harry James Orchestra. Things were clear; Sinatra showed it, and sang it loud and clear: from now on, it was all or nothing.

The heavens were manifestly on his side. Tommy Dorsey, one of the most popular jazz and swing musicians of the period, made him an offer. Sinatra had completed only six months of his two-year contract with Harry James. No matter. The singer joined Dorsey's band. Even though he knew he was losing a golden nugget, Harry James showed himself a gentleman and let his protegé go without a fuss.

Many hits followed. This period established the singer's basic repertoire, notably songs like 'I'll Never Smile Again', 'In the Blue of Evening' and 'The One I Love', which he continued to reinterpret, in different arrangements, throughout his career. In February 1940, amid the growing clamour of war, Sinatra went into the studio, at Tommy Dorsey's request, to record an unforgettable song: 'I'll Be Seeing You'. Throughout the war years, for soldiers far from their families, sailors on the high seas and pilots hunting the enemy in the skies, the song became the symbol of friends, sweethearts and loved ones left behind. From Pacific islands to the liberation of Paris, in all theatres of operations and in rough, tented camps, Sinatra's voice murmured, with that imperceptible sigh, 'I'll Be Seeing You'. He became the romantic and delicate crooner who made American women cry.

Conscious of his popularity, and playing on his personal appeal, Sinatra made the brutal decision to break with Dorsey, with no respect for the ten-year contract he had signed. His objective from that point was to build his career as a solo artist. Records, the jukebox and radio increasingly allowed solo singers to come to the fore, and relegated the bands to the background. Thirsty for fame, the singer grasped this fact immediately. Alas, Tommy Dorsey did not accept his decision with the same indulgence that Harry James had shown. As compensation, the bandleader demanded that Sinatra turn over to him 43% of his fees for a ten-year period. But Frank already had influential friends. Friends like Willie Moretti, the godfather of New Jersey. Friends in pinstripe suits and slouch hats, just the kind to make one of those notorious 'offers you can't refuse' ...

Frank Sinatra did not regret his impulse to spread his wings. In a few months, his popularity grew even further. He was sorting out recordings and tours. The concert halls were full. At every appearance of the most romantic singer of his time, impeccably attired in the latest suits and with a little bow tie below his Adam's apple, young girls fainted and teenagers wept and stomped their feet. Frank Sinatra was truly on his way. But of course, as always, he had to do everything. And a bit more.

In 1943, 'All or Nothing at All' leapt to the top of the hit parade. After the stage, after the records, Sinatra now wanted to get on the big screen, and he set his sights on Hollywood. There was no question, though, of playing supporting roles, such as in the Tommy Dorsey film where he appeared as the vocalist of the orchestra. For almost ten years, he took on the mantle of singing actor, much as Bing Crosby had done. In February 1943, he made his screen debut in Reveille with Beverly, performing Cole Porter's 'Night and Day', previously a hit for Fred Astaire.

A few films stand out among these light, made-to-measure comedies: there was *Higher and Higher* (1943), in which he co-starred with Michèle Morgan; *Anchors Aweigh* came out the following year; in 1949 there was a patriotic turn as a sailor with Gene Kelly in *On the Town* and *Take Me Out to the Ball Game*; *The Kissing Bandit* (1948); and *Double Dynamite* (1951). His most striking role, though, was certainly in the charming 1947 comedy-musical, *It Happened in Brooklyn*. All on his own, Sinatra showed himself to be voluble and cheerful. If his acting style was always casual, each of his singing scenes was a success and worked well with the comedy. Just as on stage, the singer with the blue eyes took advantage of one of the secrets of his physique: his breathing. From his debut, in fact, he had never stopped training, and had studied the techniques used by competitive swimmers. On the big screen, his 'trick' became apparent, and it was possible to discern the little opening at the corner of his lips that allowed Sinatra to breathe at the same time as he hummed or harmonised, holding the note as long as possible, holding his breath to the point of asphyxiation. This was why, throughout his career, the singer would spend as much time swimming lengths in the pool as following a score or a metronome.

His way of working was to use his charm rather than discipline. Little by little, he learned to make use of the full range of magic spells his voice could cast. The girls invariably fell at his feet. Sinatra could carry them along to the point of tears, but when they gave in and started to cry, he was already far away, carried away by the melody. To celebrate this remote being, to deepen nostalgia with soft words, to sweep away illusions without vanquishing idealism – Sinatra's style hit home. Overwhelmed by what was happening, his female fans would faint away. The singer earned a new nickname: he became 'Swoonatra', the one who made the girls black out. Who could ever imagine that his first nickname was 'Scarface' because of the scars on his left ear? The legendary animator Tex Avery, in a famous cartoon released on 15 May 1948, under the title 'Little Tinker', deliberately pulled the artist's leg by using the melody of 'All or Nothing At All'.

In October 1944, Sinatra was due to perform for the third time at the prestigious Paramount Theatre in New York. At six in the morning, there were more than a thousand people already camped out in from of the ticket counters. By nine in the morning a queue of 10,000 adolescents stretched six deep down Eighth Avenue. In Times Square, traffic was blocked and mounted police had to open a passage through the crowd. Sponsored by one of the big cigarette brands, the radio programmes went on for weeks

and weeks, captivating millions of listeners. Woody Allen's 1987 film, *Radio Days*, vividly conveys a sense of what this event was like.

Nevertheless, by the early 1950s Frank Sinatra had reached an impasse. His records were still selling, but audiences were no longer impressed. His name started appearing in smaller type on film posters. In March 1950, at the Copacabana Club in New York, there were   many empty seats. At his premieres, only the presence of Ava Gardner – then his most official girlfriend – would fill up the hall. Newspapers even began to call him 'Mr Ava Gardner' ...

Sinatra first met the actress in April 1945, in the cosy ambiance of the Mocambo nightclub, in Los Angeles. At first, he simply wanted to add 'the loveliest animal in the world' to his trophy collection. But it was he who found himself caught by the brunette with the green eyes, at the time married to actor Mickey Rooney. On one memorable night, the crooner and his friend, Jimmy Cahn, sang under the actress's window. He had several other opportunities to get to know this tall, lovely woman, who had decided to leave her North Carolina home behind to become a star. One night in 1949, during the extension of a Broadway premiere, it was love at first sight. 'We had a drink, we chatted, we fell in love,' recalled Ava Gardner some years later. They had the same tastes: the fast life, strong drink, boxing, strong sensation and Italian cooking. Frank and Ava made an explosive cocktail, and their arguments were like tropical storms.

To the press, they were the 'Battling Sinatras'. During one angry night in a suite in the Hampshire House Hotel in New York, Ava locked herself in the bedroom to get some sleep. Frank woke her by telephone. In a sepulchral voice, he said he was going to commit suicide. There was the sound of a gunshot. Ava rushed out screaming, and found his lifeless body in the other bedroom. She burst into tears, whereupon Frank opened his eyes; he had fired into a pillow to frighten her. Beside herself with an ger, she punched him before he could get up. And so it went on until the small hours of the morning. Incapable of living together, torn apart by screaming rages, they continually reconciled on more intimate terrain.

There is no doubt that he was the only man to offer this woman, so difficult to satisfy, what she had always dreamed of achieving. 'We became lovers for all time, lovers for eternity', Ava recognized, implying much. She did not display such an elegant turn of phrase during the shooting of *Mogambo* (1953) when, in front of the governor of Kenya (still a British possession at that time), she shouted to director John Ford, when he asked her what made her want to marry a 60-kilogram shortie like Frank: 'It's very simple: there's only 10 pounds of Frank, but there's 110 pounds of cock.' In short, everything worked well in the bedroom; the trouble started as soon as these two went into the bathroom. But apart from a few 'reunions', Frank was hooked. It was good a thing Ava was around, in any case, because on stage the lights were dimming. Sinatra was becoming less of a sure thing, fixed as he was in time, anchored in a particular epoch. Rock'n'roll would soon be knocking on the door, shaking things up for established solo artists. In the cinema, light comedies were still popular, but there was nothing to raise the standard. His career began to sink.

On 26 April 1950, Sinatra left the stage of the Copacabana to booing and catcalls, having completely lost his voice, the result of a haemorrhage of his vocal cords. He growled into the microphone that he was going to come down into the audience with a baseball bat. He left his self-possession in the dressing room and railed furiously against whoever got in his way. In the wings, he staggered around, ready to take on the whole world. Humiliated, the artist was a pitiful sight. He had to remain silent for forty days. He lost his grip. 'He's a dead man,' declared Swift Lazar cynically. The powerful agent had already grown weary of Sinatra's tantrums: 'In Hollywood, when you're out, you're out. Even Jesus would have missed the resurrection in this town.'

Sinatra also went too far when he made fun of Louis B Mayer's lack of height, and made jokes about Mayer's mistress, Ginny Simms. The MGM boss showed his lack of humour by terminating Sinatra's contract. Columbia followed suit, and Music Corporation of America (MCA) withdrew their support as well. His CBS television show was interrupted. Led by the pen of the redoubtable Louella Parsons, the press rushed to follow. Frank Sinatra was not in good odour in their articles. His friend Humphrey Bogart joked: 'For him, paradise is a place with only women and, above all, no journalists.'

In 1946, the Hollywood Women's Press Club awarded him the title of least cooperative star in America – a trophy of which he was most proud. From the beginning, his relations with the press were stormy, and he would even send heavies round to correct a journalist when an article made him unhappy. In November 1944, in front of the Waldorf-Astoria Hotel in New York, he came to blows with the critic Westbrook Pegler, but the matter ended there. On 10 April 1947, Lee Mortimer dragged him before the courts. *The New York Times* critic, who had attacked Sinatra for his poor acting in *It Happened in Brooklyn*, was himself violently assailed by the singer outside the fashionable Ciro's Club. Later, in front of the judge, the singer, clad in a soft tweed suit, assumed an angelic air. But that evening in front of the mic, he insulted the journalist using much more colourful and less romantic language than in his songs. Clearly, his Don Juan pin-up image took a knock. But that was Frank's way. He just couldn't shut up: 'Last night, I sang lower than usual. So low I fell in the mud. Guess what I found in the gutter? Reporters!'

His favourite victim was Dorothy Kilgallen. The Hearst writer loved to gossip about the singer's private life; in return, he used all sorts of names for her, and once sent, by messenger, a miniature gravestone with her name carved on it. One night in 1957, at the Stork Club in Los Angeles, he passed in front of the table where the journalist was sitting, wearing dark glasses. She was just about to publish *The Frank Sinatra Story*, a vitriolic biography that had provoked the singer's anger. 'Seeing what you've written, I always thought you were blind,' he shot with an evil smile, leaving

a dollar bill in front of her. Many other examples of this type punctuated his career – Elsa Maxwell, Maxine Cheshire, Barbara Walters, Dan Rather, and many others – and the costs were considerable.

For the moment, Sinatra was disparaged. Things weren't going well in his private life. No further bets. Ava Gardner, that man-eating tigress – described by Ernest Hemingway as 'superlatively feminine' – was off shooting in Spain, and was often seen on the arm of handsome hidalgos. On the set of *Pandora and the Flying Dutchman* (1951), she flirted with bullfighter Mario Cabré. The kid from Hoboken, with his Sicilian blood, was boiling mad. He set off to win her back. At the same time, he announced his divorce from Nancy and asked Ava to marry him. She hesitated. Frank knelt at her feet. Better than promises, he composed a song for her. On 27 March 1951, the singer arrived early at Capitol Records studios. Just before the recording session, he rewrote the words and changed the title. The magic worked. His voice was there. The timbre was warm, with just a little desperation, slightly rasping, helped by the romantic words and a perfect symphonic arrangement. This time it came from the heart. He sang only for Ava: 'I'm a Fool to Want You'. America cracked; the lady gave in. The wedding was set for 7 November, in Philadelphia. But two days before the ceremony, there was another earthquake. Ava slammed the door, cancelled everything, and threatened to leave. The night before, sitting at a bar with James Mason and Mason's wife, Sinatra had looked a little too meaningfully at a pretty girl. Ava threw down the engagement ring and left the establishment; shouting that the wedding was off. Frank caught up with her and saved the situation in extremis. He had no intention of letting her get away this time. In 1951, he became her third husband.

In the wedding photo, the ring shining on her left hand, Frank holds Ava around the waist while lifting the nest of tulle above her head. There was no longer any question of letting her go. His narrow face is broken by an immense smile. Ava, on the other hand, appears less striking. The brunette diva's gaze is directed elsewhere. Would Frank Sinatra be transfigured? Would the inveterate seducer metamorphose into a timid lover? It had to be believed. A happy song bore witness to this shift. Frank declared himself to be 'bewitched, lost, passionate, devoured with passion, invaded by tears'. And one night in November 1952, with no rhythm section or horns, but simply accompanied by a pianist, he gave a private concert at a small theatre in San Francisco and dedicated the song, murmuring like a bashful student: 'This is for my wife. For Ava.'

Nevertheless, people never change completely. Then came another bolt from the blue. Ava accepted a role in the film adaptation of Ernest Hemingway's *The Snows of Kilimanjaro*. Hemingway offered her the part in person. But the singer wasn't hearing out of that ear. He could not conceive that his wife could continue to pursue her career and still go off shooting overseas. Ava proposed various compromises, and even requested that her scenes be grouped together so her absence would not exceed ten days. Sinatra was furious. He was on the point of agreeing when the director indicated that eleven or twelve days would be necessary. Frank, beside himself, angrily explained that her only real role was to be the wife of Frank Sinatra. That was too much. Ava slammed the door.

1952 was the darkest year of Frank Sinatra's life. His record sales were falling, as was his radio airplay. One concert in three was cancelled. The singer let himself slide into depression, wrapped in sadness. History does not relate whether he consoled himself by listening to his own songs. He began to walk the streets, as Sammy Davis, Jr, recalled many years later: 'He was slowly walking up Broadway, with no hat, his collar open; nobody paid attention to him. I couldn't believe my eyes that this giant, who a few years before had created pandemonium in the streets, was today a simple guy just walking up the street. A guy whose friends had vanished, and he was just walking slowly along 51st Street, near the Paramount, where he had seen such success. I was going to go up to him and call him, but I understood immediately that he would not have welcomed the intrusion into his solitude.' Dark thoughts came to him, and he attempted suicide four times: once at the home of his friend Manie Sachs, vice-president of RCA Records, where he locked himself in the kitchen and turned on the gas; another time lying in the bath at the Cal Neva Lodge Hotel, where he swallowed barbiturates. Found lying on the stairs of his 57th Street home, his veins slashed open, he was rushed to Mount Sinai Hospital. In the shadows, his friend Jimmy van Heusen threw money around to keep the story quiet.

In an unexpected way, his rebirth came from Hollywood rather than from singing. Even more surprising was the fact that Ava was the instigator. The actress had heard about an excellent script, and besieged her friend Harry Cohn, the boss of Columbia Pictures. The part was supposed to go to Eli Wallach, but in Ava's eyes it was perfect for Frank. It was an opportunity not to be missed. Rumours spread that the discussions would go on late into the night ... For her thirtieth birthday, on 24 December 1952, Frank surprised Ava by joining her in Africa on the set of *Mogambo*. They were reunited once again. The gift, this time, was for him: Ava told him he was going to have a screen test. Frank flew to Hollywood.

For a fee of eight or ten thousand dollars, twenty times less than what he was earning previously, he landed the role of Private Angelo Maggio in Fred Zinnemann's *From Here to Eternity*, alongside Burt Lancaster, Montgomery Clift and Deborah Kerr. Deliriously happy, he took Ava to Paris to celebrate the news. Instead of a weekend, the couple stayed there for ten days. Zinnemann became uneasy because Sinatra had not yet arrived on set. Jokingly, the actor sent the director a telegram, boasting: 'Working on my part. STOP. On manoeuvres with the French army. STOP.' The director understood that 'working' with Sinatra was not going to be all relaxation. However, the role of the defiant, beaten-down little Italian was undoubtedly perfect for him.

The story took place amid the turmoil of Pearl Harbor just prior to the Japanese attack, weaving together human resentment, the harsh discipline of a military base and amorous intrigues. On the set, Sinatra kept a low profile behind Burt Lancaster, and got along well with Montgomery Clift. They got drunk together in the evenings in the bars of Hawaii. To the surprise of everyone, Frank was generally at work on time in the morning, looking calm and focused.

Maggio is a character with a jovial temperament, not particularly inclined to military discipline. He doesn't like injustice, but he's not really a fighter. Nevertheless, he chooses to defend his buddy against his superiors, and pays dearly for it. Sinatra offered a superbly restrained performance, with an edge of melancholy, and succeeded in highlighting the disjuncture between courage and masculinity – one of the messages of the film. Breathless, the critics applauded, and the film was an immense success. Upon receiving the Oscar for Best Supporting Actor, on 25 March 1954, Frank Sinatra, a fervent Catholic, saw it as proof of the Resurrection.

The queues in front of the cinemas stopped traffic. It was like old times. Sinatra was back – and at the top of the bill. He had no intention of going back down again. Would he have been familiar with these words of French writer André Gide?: 'It is good to follow one's own bent, so long as it leads upward.'

Whatever the case, the artist started recording again, perfecting his singing and his musical knowledge. He worked with arrangers and orchestra leaders. He became, once again, ambitious, perfectionist, obnoxious and kind.

'Young at Heart' quickly rose up the sales charts. Sinatra met again with Columbia, and at the end of 1953 negotiated a new contract with Capitol Records. His collaboration with the label was particularly fruitful. He recorded several albums under the direction of his old friend Axel Stordahl, another alumnus of the Tommy Dorsey band. Then, impressed by a Nat 'King' Cole album, he turned to Nelson Riddle. Their collaboration produced many marvellous recordings, which were certainly among the purest and fully realized of Sinatra's career. Almost all these albums passed into posterity, not just because of Sinatra but also because they added to the classic repertoire of high-quality songs that still bring success for young 'crooners' and major international artists alike. Albums such as *Songs for Young Lovers*, *A Swingin' Affair*, *Come Fly With Me*, *Swing Easy*, *In the Wee Small Hours* and *Songs for Swingin' Lovers* contained so many songs that went on to become veritable standards.

The modest Nelson Riddle knew how to bring out the best in Frank's personality by removing himself as much as possible. In all the interviews of the period, Riddle always placed the singer first, emphasizing that the songs would be nothing but sentimental fluff without the man from now on nicknamed 'The Voice'.

Galvanized by all the acclaim, Frank Sinatra decided to set up his own label. Under the imprint of Reprise Records, he recorded countless versions of his own standards, repeating youthful hits reworked by the best arrangers of the day. Nelson Riddle, as well as Robert Farnon, Neal Hefti,

Gordon Jenkins, Bill May and Axel Stordahl, all made their contribution, and special mention should be made of Quincy Jones, a newcomer with whom Sinatra established a close relationship.

Jones was a friend of Ray Charles, and made his debut in Lionel Hampton's orchestra during the mid-1950s. He made a name for himself with his warm and colourful phrasing, and especially his very modern rhythmic sense. In 1957, he moved to France, where a critical event in his development took place: he became the student of French composers Nadia Boulanger and Olivier Messiaen – like George Gershwin, Michel Legrand, Philip Glass and Leonard Bernstein before him. Quincy Jones was playing with the big boys: he became artistic director of the French label, Barclay Records, and then vice-president of Mercury, and quickly became one of the most sought-after arrangers of the period. Peggy Lee and Ella Fitzgerald swore by him. It was logical that Sinatra, who surrounded himself only with the best, would decide to work with Jones.

During the filming of *None But the Brave* (1965), Frank got bored sitting around in Hawaii. He was already thinking of a new album. One night, he decided to call Quincy Jones, whom he'd met in 1958 following a concert in Monaco. He asked him to be in Los Angeles from the following Monday for a recording session with Count Basie. In 1964, the brilliant arranger (Frank was the first to nickname him 'Q') revisited 'Fly Me to the Moon', composed ten years earlier by Bart Howard. With an ounce of rhythm, a little swing, the voice of Frank and a touch of magic, the light-hearted waltz became a hit around the world.

The story goes that during the first manned mission to the Moon, the Apollo 10 astronauts rigged up a little tape player that relayed back to NASA technicians the voice of Frank singing 'Fly Me to the Moon'. The following year, in July 1969, the commander of Apollo 11, Neil Armstrong, asked that NASA play the song for the team. At that moment, the crooner was performing live on television. When the music stopped, he reminded the audience that the real heroes were the guys in the rocket.

In return, Frank was able to grant Quincy Jones's dearest wish: to play alongside his idol, Count Basie. This took place on the stage of the Sands, in Las Vegas. Sinatra and Basie: the cover of the *Sinatra–Basie* LP gives no hint of the profound understanding that existed between these two. Wearing his best suit and that eternal hat, Frank's arms rest easily on Basie's shoulders. A relaxed, smiling Basie wears a sea captain's cap tipped back. During this period, the latter was inseparable from Frank's triumph. Whether at the piano or leading the orchestra, he was an equal partner with the soloist. Endowed with a magical sense of rhythm, Count Basie developed a fluid and complex style that was precise and sophisticated.

At the opening of the legendary concert at the Sands, recorded in 1966, over a wicked jazzy rhythm, the speaker announces to a delirious audience: 'The Sands is proud to present to you its amazing new show: a man and his music! The music of Count Basie and his big band. The man ... Frank Sinatra!' What a way to start a show! Frank came on stage, debonair as always. He began: 'What are all these people doing in my bedroom?', which drew big laughs. Then he began. The concert was magical. On the sleeve of the album, which is surely one of the finest of Sinatra's entire discography, were the two men in profile, almost juxtaposed, in the same spotlight, the same halo of triumph.

Frank Sinatra was at the peak of his art, in the full flowering of his style. His songs were luxurious and popular at the same time. Impeccably served by the finest orchestras, they murmured hope and nostalgia in the ears of Americans. Sinatra embodied once more the elegant, easy-going charmer. Style and nonchalance, romance and seduction: the cocktail certainly had its effects. His older fans envied the teenagers dancing in the aisles at his concerts. He was by now the equal of the idols of his youth, Bing Crosby and Nat 'King' Cole. More than this, Sinatra really invented the 'crooner' style. For him, the crooner was an elegant and casual singer, whom every person in the audience believed was singing just for them. From this point, Sinatra was a world star.

In 1955, his album *In the Wee Small Hours* was a best-seller for 29 weeks. In 1958, *Come Fly With Me* held the same distinction for 71 weeks. His records sold in the millions. At that moment, only Sinatra could beat Sinatra. *Only the Lonely* was a hit for more than two years – 120 weeks exactly. It was not until Michael Jackson that these records tumbled, thanks to an album produced by ... Quincy Jones.

In this context, Sinatra felt invincible, and allowed himself everything, both in public and in private. Ava Gardner had faded into the background, even if, in January 1956, Frank had recorded 'I've Got You Under My Skin'. The beauty certainly felt it, and took note of her husband's numerous affairs – Kim Novak and Judy Garland, among others. Lauren Bacall fell into the trap of thinking she was about to marry him and started signing her autograph 'Betty Sinatra'. Even Nina Krushchev, the wife of Soviet leader Nikita Krushchev, let herself be taken in when Sinatra took her hand during a gala dinner organized in Hollywood in September 1959.

Ava was cut from the same timber as he was, and she did not stick around. In Spain, during the shooting of *The Barefoot Contessa* (1954), she fell in love with the bullfighter Luis Dominguin. On 25 December, Frank surprised her by turning up in Rome, where the shooting was continuing. Drama ensued at Cinecittà studios. Frank's anger was Homeric: the television went out the window, and off he stormed. No sooner was he back in the States than he set his sights on Marilyn Monroe to make Ava angry. A divorce was granted on 5 July 1957. That very day, Sinatra was cruising on a yacht, attempting to console Lauren Bacall following the death of Humphrey Bogart. But he never erased Ava Gardner from his heart. On his estate in Palm Springs, next to the pool, he put up a statue called The Barefoot Contessa, which he had recovered from MGM studios, as a devotional shrine. A few years later, he sent her, by post, a solid-gold key that would open all the doors of his houses and apartments. In the 1980s, when the actress's health was faltering, he sent her flowers every week, visited her once a month and put his private jet at her disposal. For her part, Ava never remarried, and for the rest of her life kept in her purse a photo of her marriage to Frank.

By the early 1960s, Sinatra was everywhere triumphant, alternating between recordings, films and concerts. His favourite playground was still the stage, where he captivated audiences with his presence and his charisma. His seeming casualness, typified by the glass held in his hand, concealed a robust professionalism. He refined his style further and worked directly with the musicians. A good pianist himself, he became a remarkable trombone player and learned how to lead an orchestra. He began to introduce subtle jazz nuances into his melodies, with tempered phrasing and perfect balance between the tempo and the rhythm. He left nothing to chance. Determined to surpass Bing Crosby, he made use of all the tricks, modulating his voice and the tempo according to the melody and the words of each song. Frank Sinatra deployed the full spectrum of his magic spells.

The same was true of his big-screen career. At the end of 1955, he starred in *The Man with the Golden Arm*, with Kim Novak, and directed by Otto Preminger. It was the first film to deal seriously with the ravages of drug addiction. He convincingly brought to life the character of Frankie Machine, who is struggling with his inner demons and trying to go straight. For his performance as a man trying to halt his descent into hell, Sinatra was nominated for the Best Actor Oscar in 1955. In September 1957, he played (and sang) the role of a charming gigolo who is torn between a wise and gentle blonde, played by Kim Novak, and a rich and pushy redhead, played by Rita Hayworth, in George Sidney's film, *The Lady is a Tramp* – made famous by the song of the same name.

In the autumn of 1959, while shooting the war film *Never So Few*, Frank Sinatra and Steve McQueen found themselves on set together. Sinatra quickly assumed a paternal air toward the young actor, who had not the slightest need of such assurance. Frank took offence at this, and, always ready to play a practical joke, tossed a plaster grenade into the middle of the set, to serve as a lesson to the rookie. Pandemonium erupted. The next day, McQueen waited for Sinatra outside his dressing room, a machine pistol in his hand; he opened fire. A terrified Frank hit the ground to avoid the burst of fire. The weapon was loaded with blanks. The young man called out soberly to the crooner: 'No hard feelings, old buddy.'

By now incredibly popular, Sinatra even hosted his own weekly television show, which was sponsored by major cigarette manufacturers. His guests were people in the public eye, from Eleanor Roosevelt to the actor Cary Grant. Together with Elvis Presley, just out of the army and ill at ease in a dinner jacket, he sang 'Love Me Tender' in a jazzy arrangement put together for the occasion by his musicians. He would appear over 600 times on the small screen.

Wardrobe was a very important element in Frank Sinatra's life. In his early days, he set himself out as a fashion plate to match Bing Crosby, but then went on to create his own style. On stage he was always impeccably dressed, with just a wisp of casualness. He was extremely fastidious, insisted on the proper care of his laundry, and would change clothes several times a day. Typically, he wore a dark suit, with a carefully folded handkerchief in the breast pocket, or a tweed jacket with a slightly loosened tie. The central feature of his dressing room was, of course, the tuxedo, or dinner jacket. He had the time of his life during film shoots; in *Robin and the 7 Hoods* (1964), he famously made Sammy Davis, Jr, and Dean Martin change their suits, and even chose their ties. In the city, he wore orange jerseys – orange being his colour of choice. His private jets – Learjets bearing the initials 'FS' – presented a uniform white surface adorned with an orange stripe. His entire image was very carefully considered. Whether it was suits, shirts or cufflinks – nothing was left to chance. Under the tie, a massive gold pin secured the wings of his collar. His hats always came from Cavanagh, his shirts from Brooks Brothers. He never wore sunglasses. He had bottles of Yardley eau de Cologne specially flown over from London. On his wrist, he sported a Jager-LeCoultre Reverso watch, a gold Cartier Tank or a Royal Oak by Audemars Piguet. In one of his films, the 1957 musical *Pal Joey*, Frank was so proud of his new suit that he carried his raincoat folded over his shoulder so as to better show it off. A new fashion was immediately launched.

Once again, audiences fell at his feet, demanding more. Sinatra installed himself at the Sands together with his rowdy entourage. He may have sung for lonely hearts, but Frank was inseparable from his lively group of friends, headed by Dean Martin. This was the period of the 'Rat Pack', a group of sybarites whose motto was 'always three drinks ahead'. Although Sinatra did not invent the Rat Pack, he revived the name for the group of friends that originally came together in the 1950s around Humphrey Bogart.

Bogart fascinated Sinatra; he made friends with the star of *Casablanca*, even if he also later flirted with Lauren Bacall, Bogart's wife. Bogart soon became a sort of spiritual father, a big brother, even a Pygmalion, for Frank Sinatra. For his part, he accepted everything, and would listen to whatever Bogart said. Bogart taught him how to live, and Frank was devastated in 1957 when the older man died. For the only time in his career, he cancelled two concerts, and was so upset that he was unable to attend the funeral. The group around Bogart, which included Jimmy van Heusen, David Niven, Mike Romanoff (the celebrated Hollywood restaurateur), Swifty Lazar and Judy Garland (the sole woman), 'eased their boredom and protected their independence'. Sinatra picked up the elder's torch in the company of Dean Martin, Joey Bishop, Peter Lawford, Sammy Davis, Jr, Angie Dickinson and Shirley MacLaine. This group of millionaires would do anything to amuse themselves, and were a veritable tribe gathered round their chief. Frank was the 'Chairman of the Board', the big boss. Together, they partied late into the night. The Sands in Las Vegas was their headquarters. On stage, they passed the baton to one another, singing together, and laughing their heads off in front of an adoring audience drawn from all over the country. In the concert hall, newsmakers and politicians mingled with TV stars, mafiosi in shiny shoes, salesmen on the binge and Midwestern couples celebrating their wedding anniversaries. Let the party begin!

Frank Sinatra introduced Sammy Davis, Jr, into the Rat Pack. Davis was the first black to become a major star in the puritanical and segregated America of the 1960s. Nat 'King' Cole was a stylish singer, much in demand in the nightclubs of London and New York. But Sammy Davis, Jr, could hold the stage in front of thousands of ordinary Americans, of all backgrounds, often middle class, who came to Las Vegas to relax, have a laugh and throw away their money in the man-made desert paradise in Nevada. And even if Frank made jokes on stage that seemed racist – calling his partner 'negro', for example – the crooner, the 'Wop from Hoboken', knew something about bringing down barriers.

Nothing could stop the Rat Pack, in public or in private. Always up for a party, the Chairman of the Board dragged his supporting cast along on innumerable all-nighters. Life began at 9pm. Girls, known by the generic term of 'broads', would parade around. Frank kept three rooms at the Sands for use after his concerts. A girl waited in the rooms on either side of his own: a blonde in the left-hand room, a brunette on the right. At the last minute he would choose (on the nights when he chose …). Everything was a big joke. Death was nicknamed 'The Big Casino'. Jack Daniel's, Frank's favourite drink, flowed in torrents; they called it 'gasoline'. One of his three jets – one dubbed 'Tina' (like his daughter), another El Dago – was always ready for take-off. The limousines were as long as the night.

Sinatra and his friends had an easy life, and ran from any kind of pressure. Sinatra no longer wanted to exert himself on screen. On the big screen, the Rat Pack films were light-hearted fluff, and showed a bunch of kids playing together, just like at school. 'Let's play cowboys or gangsters', Sinatra seems to say from the first scene. Ocean's 11 (1960) was the ultimate expression. During the filming, Sinatra would have spray-gun fights with Dean Martin, or the two partners in crime would take off before the end of the scene. If the director became too 'directorial', Sinatra would silence him with his big-chief air. He would accept suggestions, but not orders. The same principle applied to concert tours. Some nights on stage at the Sands, the performers chatted for longer than they sang. They drank and smoked on stage. Dean Martin looked like he was drunk; Sammy Davis, Jr, was the official jester; Peter Lawford affected an air of boredom, no doubt to seem more British.

Nevertheless, there were moments of grace. In an episode that marked his life until its end, he recorded 'Strangers in the Night' on 11 April 1966. Recorded quickly, in a single take, the song was at first intended as the B-side of a 45-rpm single. A local radio station began to play it; their switchboard went crazy because so many listeners wanted to hear it. In one afternoon, the station broadcast the song 17 times. The romantic ditty, one of the most vapid and conventional, soon became a worldwide hit.

The orchestration was average, the arrangement simplistic, but Sinatra would sing it his whole life. He would invariably turn to his musicians and grumble about the composer. However, the song contributed much to the singer's immense fortune and to the 120 million records sold in the course of his career.

On 19 July 1966, Sinatra married Mia Farrow while the song played. To everyone's surprise, the fifty-something singer had fallen in love with this skinny, androgynous 19-year-old. He took her on a cruise aboard a huge yacht, leaving behind the rest of the 'family'. Dean Martin accordingly declared that he owned a whisky that was older than her. But once his ardour was spent, Frank became impossible again and went back to his old buddies. Then, in April 1967, the party was over. The Sands was bought by billionaire Howard Hughes, who thanked everyone for their efforts. But Frank would never agree to go on the payroll of his enemy, and proceeded to sign a contract with Caesar's Palace, just to be contrary.

Beyond the sequins and the glamour, the entertainment business often had a rotten side. If Sinatra played the role of private detective Tony Rome on screen, some of his off-screen associations were fairly dubious.

Sinatra's family came from the Sicilian town of Lercara Friddi (like Salvatore Lucana, better known as 'Lucky Luciano'), located between Corleone and Prizzi, and he associated with gangsters from an early age. His mother Dolly was already building up links within this very influential milieu. It was thanks to her, notably, that he was able to make his debut as a singer, and that many of the charges made against him were miraculously dropped. On 11 February 1947, the singer went so far as to pose for photos with Lucky Luciano, his 'compatriot', at the Hotel Nacional in Havana, Cuba. Following the death of Marilyn Monroe in 1962, it was no coincidence that her husband, Joe DiMaggio, barred both the singer and Peter Lawford from attending the funeral. Some days previously, the troubled star had spent a weekend with the two buddies at the Cal Neva Lodge, which was owned by Sinatra himself. On the other hand, when his own son was kidnapped, on 8 December 1963, Frank was beside himself and roused the entire West Coast, including his 'friends', to come to the rescue. Attorney General Robert Kennedy took the affair very seriously, contacted the singer personally and ordered 150 FBI agents to comb the Lake Tahoe area. From his side, the mafia don Sam Giancana offered his own 'special services': a ransom of $240,000 was quietly paid to the kidnappers. After this generous gesture, Sinatra showed himself obliging and ready to serve. At the Sands, he would finish his set with the song 'My Kind of Town (Chicago Is)', the royalties from which were paid directly to the syndicate.

Frank Sinatra never hesitated to rough up any journalist who dared to suggest a link between him and the Mafia. A notable case occurred in April 1976, following the publication of a photo showing him backstage at the Westchester Premier Theater, in the charming company of mobsters Carlo Gambino, Paul Castellano and 'Jimmy the Weasel' Fratianno. Francis

Ford Coppola was also the source of one of Sinatra's legendary rages, after the director took Sinatra as the inspiration for the character of Johnny Fontane, the crooner who sings at the wedding of Don Corleone's daughter, in *The Godfather* (1971).

Nevertheless, as surprising as it may seem, discretion never seems to have been a priority for Sinatra. From this perspective, the film *Robin and the 7 Hoods* takes the form of a veritable confession shot in Cinemascope. Following the discovery of the body of Sam Giancana, executed in the cellar of his home in Oak Park, Illinois, in June 1975, the singer began to attract the attention of prosecutors …

And what of Sinatra's shady friends? John F Kennedy knew all about them, but preferred to shut his eyes. The whole Kennedy clan knew about it, in fact, and there were several who protested. Jackie Kennedy was prominent in not showing support for Frank. However, Sinatra was fascinated by the President. He became heavily engaged in Kennedy's election campaign, at a time when artists were still highly circumspect about publicizing their political opinions. The Rat Pack was even renamed the 'Jack Pack' for the duration of the campaign. Certainly, Frank performed during the election night gala, rewriting the words of one of his songs, which became 'That Old Jack Magic'. But there was no question of ascending to the rostrum during the inauguration. He who had been so accommodating over the years – from raising funds for the campaign to filling the candidate's bed (notably presenting Kennedy with the lovely Judith Campbell, who also happened to be the mistress of godfather Sam Giancana) – was pushed aside. In addition, he was barred from access to his most cherished dream: to become US ambassador to Italy.

In March 1962, hoping to rebuild his relationship with Kennedy, Sinatra invited the President to spend the weekend at his Palm Springs estate. After the invitation was accepted in principle, the whole place was hastily repainted, including the room where Frank kept his model trains and aircraft and his many trophies, surrounded by a collection of photos from the 1940s. 'Jack' had visited once before, on 5–6 November 1960 – immediately prior to the presidential election. Sinatra had mounted a copper commemorative plaque on the door of the bedroom used by Kennedy, but typically got the dates wrong. A temporary structure was quickly erected in the garden to accommodate the President's bodyguards, and a flagpole was put up to fly the Stars and Stripes. The entire neighbourhood was warned about the visit, but the guest never arrived. At the last moment, Robert Kennedy, the President's brother and US Attorney General, advised strongly against the visit. He asked his brother-in-law, Peter Lawford, to act as a go-between to break the news to Frank. The latter never spoke another word to his Rat Pack buddy. Sinatra's humiliation was complete when, at the last minute, Kennedy chose to spend the weekend with Bing Crosby, a Republican.

On 22 November 1963, the day of President Kennedy's assassination, Sinatra was shocked but also uneasy. In 1954, in the film *Suddenly*, directed by Lewis Allan, he played a contract killer hired by the Mafia to kill the President of the United States. For Sinatra, the odour of scandal was a little too strong, and he took steps to block distribution of the film. Ready to throw fuel on the fire, journalists reported that Lee Harvey Oswald had watched the film a few days before opening fire on Kennedy's Lincoln convertible in Dallas.

By the beginning of the 1970s, the crooner's star had once more begun to wane. He was recording less, contenting himself with doing duets and re-recordings. His voice was still strong, and his lapels widened with the times, but his style was growing out of fashion. At the height of the hippie period, when even John Lennon wore psychedelic Indian jackets, Sinatra decided to counter-attack. He divorced Mia Farrow. On 30 December 1968, he picked up a song by French singer-songwriter Claude François. It was rush-released in early 1969 and 'My Way' became a massive success, eclipsing even Woodstock. Sinatra still had it.

On 7 April 1970, the singer was chosen to present a special Oscar to Cary Grant, in celebration of his career as an actor. On 13 June 1971, before an audience of astounded celebrities at the Los Angeles Music Center, he announced his retirement. Ronald Reagan and the Prince and Princess of Monaco were there, together with the cream of Hollywood. Henry Kissinger sat next to Elizabeth Taylor. Frank Sinatra said his goodbyes – for the first time.

In April 1973 he was back behind the mic. This time he really put his foot in it: he sang at Richard Nixon's second inaugural gala. Even though he was a fervent Democrat (as his mother had been) and had taken an active part in the presidential campaigns of Roosevelt and Kennedy, he now changed sides. He began to campaign actively for Ronald Reagan, who was running for governor of California, no doubt hoping for a position in his entourage. Because he was fascinated by power, the crooner loved politics. In February 1965, he was in raptures after French president Charles de Gaulle decorated him. Following the election of Ronald Reagan to the White House in 1980, Sinatra organized the inaugural gala, and placed himself in the second row for the swearing of the oath of office. During the ovations, Reagan ascended to the rostrum. Nancy Reagan, in a green suit, held Reagan's hand. Frank, wearing an onyx signet ring and a silver tie, never shifted his gaze. This time there was no question of staying in the shadows, as in 1961. The programme for that evening's performance, which was entitled 'The Beginning of a Great New Beginning', listed Frank as no less than producer, director and artistic director of the event. The list of artists he had invited was long and prestigious; to the sounds of the Don Costa Orchestra appeared Dean Martin, Johnny Carson, Debby Boone, Bob Hope, Mel Tillis and … Frank Sinatra. On 19 June 1989, for the inauguration of President George Bush, Sinatra was again on the programme. On 29 November 1989, he received a letter from the White House to mark his 75th birthday. George and Barbara Bush were two weeks early with their greetings, but they absolutely wanted to be first.

In spite of his age, Sinatra had neither had his last word nor sung his last romantic song. He was the headliner at a concert in Madison Square Garden on 13 October 1974, dubbed 'The Main Event'. And so it began all over again. Barbara Blakely, recently divorced from Zeppo Marx, became his third wife in 1976. He gave her a white Rolls-Royce as a wedding gift; she chose a Jaguar 'E' Type for him. But Sinatra didn't much like to drive. If he was seen from time to time at the wheel of an elegant 1958 Cadillac Eldorado Brougham, a sporty Ford Thunderbird or the baroque Stutz Blackhawk – and on screen taking Grace Kelly for a spin in a Mercedes 190 SL – he really loved big American limousines. He much preferred a chauffeur-driven Lincoln or a Cadillac as long as a poker game with his buddies. One legendary car was the orange Lamborghini Miura LP 400 that belonged to his son-in-law; Sinatra had fun driving it around a few times, as he did the Maserati Ghibli that belonged to his daughter Tina's husband. But a few years later the car was painted orange in an effort to boost the price at auction. The cost of maintaining all his limousines, private jets and luxurious homes forced Frank Sinatra to keep touring. And so the adventure continued.

And so the artist set out on another world tour. Seemingly inexhaustible, he signed another contract with Caesar's Palace in Las Vegas. Nothing seemed to hold him back or to affect him. Nevertheless, in January 1977, he cried in public for the first time. His mother's funeral was a relatively private affair; Dean Martin and Jimmy van Heusen were among the pallbearers. Dolly was killed in a plane crash in the San Gregorio Mountains, on the way to Las Vegas to hear her son sing. (By a strange coincidence, Dean Martin's son died at the controls of a jet aircraft in the same area in 1988.) It took Frank several days to regain his composure. At his father's death, on 24 January 1969, his face looked like marble. The show must go on.

In September 1979, at the invitation of the wife of Egyptian president Anwar el-Sadat, Frank Sinatra joined fifty other musicians in a massive charity concert at the foot of the Pyramids of Giza. The initiative for the event came from Jacques Bergerac, a native of Biarritz, who had worked as an actor in Hollywood during the 1950s. Bergerac had appeared with Audrey Hepburn in Vincente Minnelli's *Gigi* (1958), was celebrated for his marriages, first to Ginger Rogers and then to Dorothy Malone, and had gone on to become president of cosmetics giant Revlon. By now with Pierre Balmain, Bergerac was looking for a striking way to launch the perfume 'Ivoire', and so Sinatra made himself available. Tickets for the event went for more than $150 each. The audience were seated on the ground on thousands of Persian carpets. As always, Sinatra turned sand into gold: the event brought in more than one million dollars. That afternoon, Sinatra had visited the Faith and Hope Rehabilitation Center, a hospital for orphans from the Six Day War (1967) located in a suburb of Cairo. Side by side with Gehane el-Sadat, and with celebrated French photographer Jean-Daniel Lorieux recording the event, Sinatra watched the young patients sit up in their beds while singing 'Strangers in the Night', even though his songs had

been banned in Egypt since 1962, when he performed in Israel. During a dinner for 850 guests, lit by pink candles and surrounded by models sent by Pierre Balmain, the President's wife declared that the evening was 'one of the historic events that has marked the five-thousand-year history of the Sphinx'. Sinatra was struck dumb.

On 12 December 1979, Sinatra was the guest of honour at a grand evening organized by NBC at Caesar's Palace in Las Vegas. Don Costa led the orchestra, and 'The Voice' did his thing, singing five songs and hearing a slew of artists interpret his standards. They were all there: Dean Martin and Sammy Davis, Jr, his old friends; his children Nancy, Frank and Tina, to lead the dance. And many others answered 'present': Harry James, Jimmy van Heusen, Sammy Cahn, Robert Merrill, Tony Bennett – 'the singer's singer' – all took part. Gene Kelly needed no coaxing; Julio Iglesias, a son in spirit, was filled with emotion. Cary Grant did not sing, but came out with wonderful compliments that reflected his usual good humour and elegance. Paul Anka was moved; Lucille Ball was still radiant. They all came for him. Sinatra savoured his triumph from his patriarch's armchair. 'All or Nothing at All.' When NBC broadcast the show on 3 January 1980, all of America tuned in to relive the dream.

Nevertheless, things started to go wrong. The singer would arrive late for shows, or could not always finish his songs. The audience would whisper the words to him. Even so, 'Mack the Knife', from the album *L.A. is My Lady*, became a hit. In 1984, Sinatra was taken ill during a concert tour. Even the Grammy Legend Award he received in 1994 in honour of his long career left him rather unmoved. He spent more and more time in Monaco. Beside the pool at the Beach Club, he covered himself with sun lotion, adjusted his hairpiece and tanned himself to the sounds of a portable radio. Before she died in 1982, Grace Kelly often invited him over, as a way of raising the public profile of the principality. She had been his co-star in *High Society* in 1956, during Hollywood's golden age. It had been Grace Kelly's last film, and had also starred Bing Crosby and Louis Armstrong. And for once, he sat down with a journalist. In 1986 he guest-starred on the television series 'Magnum, P.I.', alongside Tom Selleck, in an episode entitled 'Laura'. It was to be his last appearance on camera.

In 1988, when he got the idea of reforming the Rat Pack, his heart wasn't in it. If Sammy Davis, Jr, appeared faithfully beside Sinatra, Dean Martin backed out after a week. Liza Minnelli tried to fill in for him for a final few concerts, but the evidence was clear: all bets were off. The press mocked the 'Together Again Tour'. During the London concert, which took place at the Royal Albert Hall, a 77-year-old woman, beautiful in former days but marked by two strokes and the effects of gin and cigarettes, took a seat where she would not be recognized. She applauded Liza Minnelli and Sammy Davis, Jr, but her almond eyes lit up only when the man she had been waiting for took the stage. When she got home after the show, she telephoned Frank in his hotel suite. Without introducing herself, she said soberly: 'You've still got an exceptional voice, Frankie.' Speechless with surprise and emotion, the singer instantly recognized Ava Gardner's voice.

On Tuesday 25 April 1989, at the moment when the protesters were gathering in Beijing's Tiananmen Square, Sinatra went on stage at the Paris Opera House. It was 8pm exactly; his contract demanded it, just like the piano and the bottle of vintage Bordeaux in his dressing room. Frank was always insufferable like this. The posters announced 'The Ultimate Event!' and the cream of Parisian society toasted him with Champagne. Sinatra made fun of the whole thing, and started to sing to two empty rows of seats. A couple of hours previously, the mayor of Paris, Jacques Chirac, had honoured the celebrated singer, icon of a certain happy image of America, with a gold medal and a reception worthy of a head of state. Speaking before an audience of celebrities and important business figures, the mayor spoke of his own admiration for the singer. The speech, given in English in the accent of the Corrèze region of central France, was rich: 'Let me tell you, in my poor English, that you will never be a stranger. Even in the night.' The audience laughed uproariously. Always that blasted song.

The halls were full in Europe, in Australia and in Japan, and tickets changed hands for high prices. Frank was certainly at the top of the bill, his name printed ten times larger than anyone else. But his gestures were less precise: he lacked spirit, and his voice was no longer there.

The singer had often lent his image to advertising, and had given his name to a brand of pasta sauce. He understood early the appeal of these associated products. In the 1960s, he posed for a celebrated brand of Havana cigars, although he himself didn't smoke. The trinkets that bore his name were as numerous as they were often improbable: an alarm clock, golf balls, Japanese bottled beer. In 1981, with the singer's blessing, Chrysler had marketed a limited edition of the Imperial, his favourite model, baptized 'FS'. The bodywork was blue, like his eyes. Some 278 of these cars were produced, complete with a cabinet, built in under the dashboard and car radio, made from expensive wood and containing an anthology of Sinatra's finest songs on ten cassettes ... Happily, we still have his albums.

'I hope that you live to be 100 and that the last thing you hear is my voice.' In 1993, Capitol Records provided the means to realize Sinatra's wish, issuing an anthology of 30 years of recordings on the Reprise Records label. The publicity material announced 'the musical event of the decade'. The magic was working once again. On 14 October 1993, with the help of all the tricks offered by technology, the artist launched a series of duets with the greatest stars in show business: Aretha Franklin, Carly Simon, Barbra Streisand, Tony Bennett, Charles Aznavour, Julio Iglesias, Willie

Nelson, Natalie Cole, Kenny G and Bono. The crooner style came back into fashion, and Capitol encouraged Sinatra to pursue the project. A second album of duets was released in 1994. Stevie Wonder, Antonio Carlos Jobim, Chrissie Hynde, Lena Horne and even Gladys Knight all wanted to sing with 'Ol' Blue Eyes'. Sinatra was not really in shape for singing, but technicians kept the magic alive.

On 19 and 20 December 1994, at the Fukuoka Dome in Tokyo, Sinatra gave his last concert, directed by his son. He appeared on stage again on 25 February 1995, but there was no longer any question of singing. He gave a fundraising speech during the annual charity gala of his wife's foundation, the Barbara Sinatra Children's Center. A golf tournament in Palm Springs that same year was his last public appearance.

In December that year, a tribute evening was organized at the Shrine Auditorium in Los Angeles. Barbara had announced in advance that her husband would not be able to participate. He retired to his house in Rancho Mirage, California, at 70-588 Frank Sinatra Drive. What a road he had travelled from Monroe Street in Hoboken! ABC broadcast a live concert entitled 'Sinatra: 80 Years My Way'; musicians like Ray Charles, Tony Bennett, Natalie Cole, Bob Dylan, Little Richard, Bruce Springsteen and Vic Damone, as well as actors Robert Wagner, Gregory Peck and Johnny Depp, all paid tribute to him during the 90-minute special. The show broke audience records. America was at his feet once more. In 1997, the Congress of the United States awarded him its Gold Medal for the body of his work.

On 15 May 1998, silence fell in a large room in the Cedars-Sinai Medical Center in Los Angeles. During the night, in a gesture of reverence, with the Empire State Building illuminated in blue, the casinos of Las Vegas dimmed their lights and the landmark Capitol Tower in Los Angeles was symbolically draped in black. On the day of the funeral, fighter jets wrote the letters F and S in the sky, while President Bill Clinton handed over an American flag to Barbara, an honour usually reserved for military personnel. All or Nothing at All.

Frank Sinatra was dead, and America was left orphaned. The crooner's sings had formed the soundtrack to the 20th century. His epitaph, engraved for posterity upon his tombstone, reprises one of his greatest hits: 'The Best is Yet to Come'.

Frédéric Brun

'I'm going to live till I die.'

Frank Sinatra

1921 / Frank Sinatra, aged 5.

1920 / Frank Sinatra's childhood home in Hoboken, New Jersey.

1923 / Frank Sinatra, aged 7, on the day of his first communion.

1924 / Frank Sinatra, aged 8.

1933 / Portrait of Frank Sinatra, aged 17.

1922 / The Sinatra family at Echo Farm House, in the Catskill Mountains of New York State. The young Frank, aged 6, is shown seated in the first row, on the right.

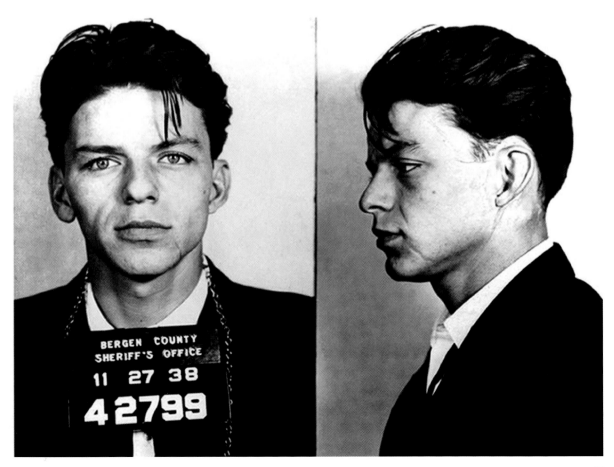

1938 / Sinatra, 22, was arrested by police in Bergen, New Jersey, and charged with 'seduction under the promise of marriage' to 'a single female of good repute for chastity'. He was released with a warning after the intervention of his mother and some friends from the 'neighbourhood'.

1938 / After making his name initially in modest bars and restaurants, Sinatra joined The Hoboken Four, shown here at the NBC recording studios. Together they won a talent competition that allowed them to tour with the Major Bowes Travelling Show.

1938 / Frank Sinatra, shown in the first row (third from right), joined the Harry James Orchestra as a vocalist, together with Connie Haines. His self-confidence –
he was already calling himself the 'greatest singer' – brought him his first press notices.

'Luck is fine, and you have to have luck to get the opportunity. But after that, you've got to have talent and know how to use it.'

Frank Sinatra

1944 / On 3 May, Sinatra appears at Hunter College, in New York City, for a radio broadcast.

24

1944 / Aged 27, Frank Sinatra appears on stage at the Riobamba nightclub in New York City.

1940 / While war raged in Europe, the 25-year-old Sinatra recorded 'I'll Be Seeing You'. The song, which spoke of loved ones far away, was later adopted by servicemen in all theatres of operations, as well as by their sweethearts and families back in the States. Frank instantly became an enormous star, breaking many hearts.

ALL OR NOTHING AT ALL

Words and Music by
JACK LAWRENCE and ARTHUR ALTMAN
A.S.C.A.P.   A.S.C.A.P.

FEATURED ON COLUMBIA RECORDS
BY **FRANK SINATRA**

WITH **HARRY JAMES**
AND HIS ORCHESTRA

Leeds Music

1943 / The song 'All or Nothing At All', written in 1939 by Jack Lawrence to music by Arthur Altman, leapt to the top of the hit parade. The title fit Sinatra like a glove, because the crooner wanted it all: fame, women, an acting career, money, friends in high places ... he would have all of these, and more.

'I was giving back to those girls all the love they gave me. They wrote me thousands of letters, and everytime I sang, I made love to them.'

Frank Sinatra

1947 / Portrait of Frank Sinatra, aged 31.

1943 / Frank Sinatra and his daughter Nancy (born 8 June 1940) at home in New Jersey.

1943 / Frank Sinatra, his first wife Nancy Barbato and their daughter Nancy, in the kitchen of the family home. In February that year, the crooner appeared in *Reveille With Beverly*, directed by Charles Barton. It was Sinatra's first screen credit.

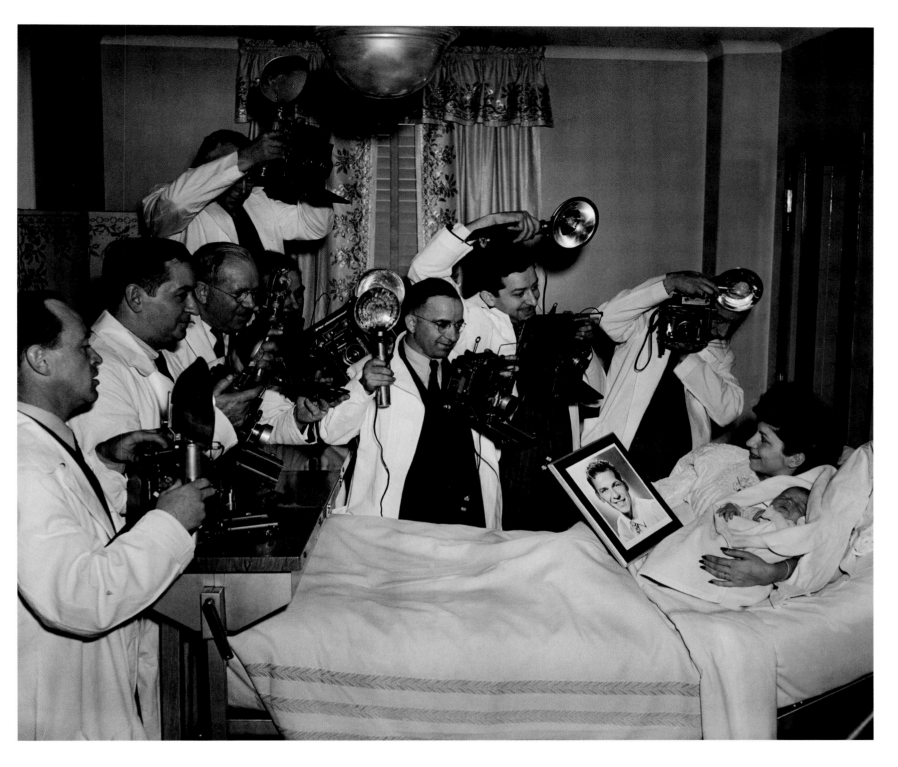

1944 / Frank Sinatra plays with his daughter Nancy, then aged 4. Many years later, their shared passion for singing produced 'Somethin' Stupid' (1967), a song that eventually rose to number one on the Billboard chart.

1944 / The day after the birth of Frank, Jr, reporters were at the bedside of Nancy Sinatra in her room at Margaret Hague Maternity Hospital, in Jersey City.

1948 / Frank Sinatra with Nancy Barbato and their children, Nancy and Frank, Jr, at the piano.

1947 / Frank Sinatra with his family at the Stork Club, in New York. Sinatra was 23 when he married Nancy Barbato, on 4 February 1939. Throughout their marriage, which lasted until 1951, he never attempted to conceal his extramarital affairs, but was nevertheless a considerate father.

'In Hoboken, when I was a kid, I lived in a plenty tough neighborhood. When somebody called me a "dirty little pig", there was only one thing to do: break his head. When I got older, I realized you shouldn't do it [get even] that way. I realized you've got to do it through education . . . maybe with a few exceptions.'

Frank Sinatra

1947 / Frank Sinatra poses for a publicity campaign. In April of the same year, the singer – who was used to scandals – had come to blows with journalist Lee Mortimer, who had been rude about him in a newspaper column.

38

1949 / Poster for the musical *On the Town*, directed by Stanley Donen and Gene Kelly. The hit film told the story of three Navy sailors, Gabey (Gene Kelly), Chip (Frank Sinatra) and Ozzie (Jules Munshin), who disembark in New York for a day's shore leave.

1949 / Frank Sinatra and Gene Kelly were the headliners in *On the Town*, which won the 1950 Academy Award for Best Music, Scoring of a Musical Picture.

1953 / Poster for the film *From Here to Eternity*, directed by Fred Zinnemann.

1953 / The year 1953 was catastrophic for Frank Sinatra: record sales slumped and concerts were cancelled. Sinatra fell into a depression, and needed to bounce back. Salvation came via his second wife, Ava Gardner, who lobbied with Harry Cohn, the boss of Columbia Pictures, to secure for him the role of Sergeant Maggio in *From Here to Eternity*. For one-twentieth of his old salary, Sinatra landed the part, working alongside Montgomery Clift and Burt Lancaster.

1953 / Director Fred Zinnemann gives directions to Montgomery Clift and Frank Sinatra on the set of *From Here to Eternity*. The film was an enormous success in cinemas, and went on to win eight Oscars in 1954: Best Film, Best Director, Best Screenplay, Best Cinematography, Best Sound, Best Film Editing, Best Supporting Actor (Frank Sinatra) and Best Supporting Actress (Donna Reed).

1953 / Burt Lancaster, Frank Sinatra and Ernest Borgnine enjoy a moment of relaxation on set at Columbia Pictures studios.

'We became lovers for all time, lovers for eternity.'

Ava Gardner

1951 / On 7 November, Frank Sinatra, aged 36, married Ava Gardner. Inseparable as lovers, they had a passionate relationship that was marked by tumultuous arguments and numerous reconciliations.

1953 / Ava Gardner and Frank Sinatra were one of the most famous couples in Hollywood. Even if their turbulent union officially lasted just six years, the two remained on good terms until the actress's death in 1990.

'The best revenge is massive success.'

Frank Sinatra

1954 / During the Oscar ceremony, *From Here to Eternity*, directed by Fred Zinnemann, garnered eight golden statuettes, with the awards including Best Supporting Actor for Frank Sinatra and Best Supporting Actress for Donna Reed. The cast and crew celebrated this achievement in style at Romanoff's restaurant, in Los Angeles.

FRANK SINATRA · ELEANOR PARKER · KIM NOVAK

THE MAN WITH THE GOLDEN ARM

A film by Otto Preminger

an 'untouchable' theme...an unusual motion picture!

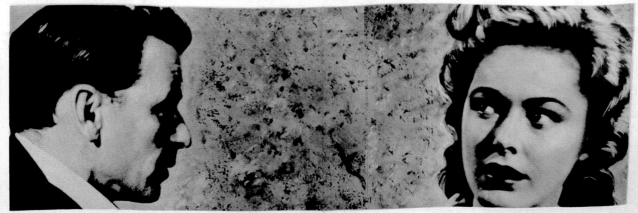

With Arnold Stang, Darren McGavin, Robert Strauss, John Conte, Screenplay by Walter Newman & Lewis Meltzer, From the novel by Nelson Algren, Music by Elmer Bernstein, Produced & Directed by Otto Preminger A United Artists Release

1955 / American poster for the film *The Man With the Golden Arm*, directed by Otto Preminger.

1955 / Frank Sinatra, aged 39, played the role of Frankie Machine in *The Man With the Golden Arm*.

1955 / Frank Sinatra, shown here at RKO Studios, learned to play the drums for the role of Frankie Machine, a former drug addict who discovers he has a talent for drumming, in Otto Preminger's *The Man With the Golden Arm*.

1955 / *The Man With the Golden Arm* was the first Hollywood production to deal with the problem of drugs and their effects. The film earned three Oscar nominations in 1956: Best Actor for Frank Sinatra, Best Musical Direction for Joseph C Wright and Darrell Silvera, and Best Original Score for Elmer Bernstein.

1956 / American poster for *High Society*, directed by Charles Walters. The film received two Oscar nominations, in the categories of Best Music, Scoring of a Musical Picture, and Best Song (Cole Porter's 'True Love').

1956 / For *High Society*, Frank Sinatra shared top billing with Grace Kelly, Celeste Holm and Bing Crosby, whose multifarious career he had admired since adolescence.

1956 / *High Society* was a remake of the 1940 film *The Philadelphia Story*, directed by George Cukor, which had starred Katherine Hepburn, Cary Grant and James Stewart. It was Grace Kelly's last feature film before she became The Princess of Monaco.

'He was the epitome of what singing is all about, beautiful sounds, smooth as silk, effortless, impeccable phrasing, stylish, intelligent and full of heart.'

Barbra Streisand

1952 / Portrait of Frank Sinatra, aged 36. Always impeccably dressed, the incomparable crooner, nicknamed 'The Voice', made use of his charisma and natural elegance to seduce America.

1959 / American poster for the film *Never So Few*, directed by John Sturges, which brought together Frank Sinatra, Gina Lollobrigida, Peter Lawford and Steve McQueen.

1959 / Frank Sinatra and Steve McQueen during the filming of *Never So Few*. The singer was quite patronizing towards the young actor, who didn't appreciate this. On the set, they provoked one another with tough-guy practical jokes. The crooner once lobbed a plaster grenade at McQueen just as he was getting ready to play a scene. The actor responded the following day, machine pistol in hand, firing a burst of blanks as Sinatra left his dressing room.

1960 / Poster for the musical comedy *Can-Can*. The film, which told the story of Simone Pistache, director and producer of revues at the cabaret Le Bal De Paradis, in Montmartre, achieved considerable success. Notably, in 1961 the film received a Grammy Award for Best Original Soundtrack, for Cole Porter's songs.

1959 / Frank Sinatra starred in *Can-Can* alongside Shirley MacLaine and Maurice Chevalier. The film was directed by Walter Lang.

1959 / During a break in filming, Sinatra discusses a point with the director and production crew at 20th Century Fox studios.

1954 / Portrait of Frank Sinatra, aged 38, taken during a recording session in Los Angeles.

'I'm a performer. I'm better in the first take.'

Frank Sinatra

1959 / Inside 20th Century Fox studios, Frank Sinatra goes over his script on the set of the film *Can-Can*, directed by Walter Lang.

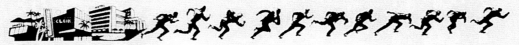

1960 / American poster for the film *Ocean's 11*, directed by Lewis Milestone, and starring Frank Sinatra, Dean Martin, Sammy Davis, Jr, Peter Lawford and Angie Dickinson. The film would be remade in 2001 by director Steven Soderbergh, starring George Clooney, Brad Pitt, Matt Damon and Julia Roberts.

1960 / *Ocean's 11* told the story of the robbery of a Las Vegas casino by a group of expert thieves, played by four of the 'Rat Pack' – Sammy Davis, Jr, Dean Martin, Frank Sinatra and Joey Bishop. The film was made on their turf, just a short distance from the Sands Club, where they appeared on stage.

1960 / Portrait of Frank Sinatra, aged 44, outside the prestigious Sands Club, in Las Vegas.

1960 / Frank Sinatra poses for a showgirl at the Sands, in Las Vegas, during his appearance with the Rat Pack under the banner of the famous 'Summit Meeting'.

'I can't help myself: I'm for anything that gets you through the night, be it prayer, tranquilizers, or a bottle of Jack Daniel's.'

Frank Sinatra

1957 / Promotional photo for the film *Pal Joey*, directed by George Sidney. The film told the story of nightclub singer who has to choose between a smart younger woman (the blonde Kim Novak) and a fabulously wealthy, provocative older woman (the readhead Rita Hayworth). A true dandy, Sinatra decided to wear his trench coat folded over his shoulder to better display his suit. He immediately started a fashion.

1963 / Flanked by Nancy Sinatra, his mother, Frank Sinatra, Jr, answers reporters' questions following his abduction in the Lake Tahoe area three days earlier.

1963 / Frank Sinatra takes part in a press conference relating to the kidnapping of his 19-year-old-son, on 8 December 1963. Frank, Jr, was released after his father paid a ransom of $240,000.

1960 / Portrait of Frank Sinatra, aged 44, at his home in Palm Springs.

1960 / John F Kennedy and Frank Sinatra pose together in Las Vegas, where the presidential candidate had come to campaign. The crooner was fascinated by political power, and by Kennedy in particular. He gave massive support to the Kennedy campaign, and even renamed the Rat Pack the 'Jack Pack' for the occasion.

'Last night, I sang lower than usual. So low I fell in the mud. Guess what I found in the gutter? Reporters!'

Frank Sinatra

1960 / Portrait of Frank Sinatra, aged 44, taken during the Democratic National Convention, in Los Angeles.

SINATRA-BASIE

AN HISTORIC MUSICAL FIRST

1962 / Cover of the album *Sinatra–Basie*, arranged by Quincy Jones, which marked a turning point in the 'Sinatra sound'.

1962 / Surrounding himself with only the very best, Sinatra contacted Quincy Jones, an arranger-producer of genius, to work with him on a new album. The sessions initiated the magical partnership with Count Basie, and the trio gave life to a legendary album.

1962 / Good humour was the rule in the recording studio: Frank Sinatra has fun here with a badge urging him to practise harder.

1962 / Frank Sinatra records, accompanied by a prestigious orchestra led by Count Basie at the piano.

1959 / Frank Sinatra records *Come Dance With Me*, which became the most popular album of his career. It stayed on the Billboard chart for two-and-a-half years (140 weeks), and won various Grammy Awards in 1960 (Album of the Year, Best Male Vocal Performance and Best Arrangements, for Billy May).

1959 / Frank Sinatra works with composer Nelson Riddle during the recording of the album *Come Dance With Me*.

'Whatever else has been said about me personally is unimportant. When I sing, I believe I'm honest.'

Frank Sinatra

1966 / Frank Sinatra, aged 50, was one of the stars of the epic *Cast a Giant Shadow*, a war film inspired by the life of the Colonel David Marcus, a Jewish American who set up the Israeli armed forces in Palestine.

LA COMPAGNIE MIRISCH
présente

L'OMBRE
D'UN GEANT
(CAST A GIANT SHADOW)

AVEC KIRK
DOUGLAS
YUL
BRYNNER
SENTA
BERGER

ET AVEC
ANGIE DICKINSON · JAMES DONALD
STATHIS GIALLELIS · LUTHER ADLER
AVEC LA PARTICIPATION DE
FRANK SINATRA
JOHN WAYNE (LE GENERAL)

Un film de
MELVILLE SHAVELSON
Écrit pour l'écran et réalisé par MELVILLE SHAVELSON
Producteur associé MICHAEL WAYNE
Musique ELMER BERNSTEIN · Produit par Mirisch · Lienroc · Batjac
TECHNICOLOR® PANAVISION®

1966 / Poster for the film *Cast a Giant Shadow*, directed by Melville Shaveleson, which brought together Kirk Douglas, Yul Brynner, Frank Sinatra, John Wayne and Senta Berger.

1966 / In *Cast a Giant Shadow*, Sinatra played a supporting role beside Kirk Douglas, whose son Michael played his first role in the film.

1965 / Frank Sinatra starred as Colonel Joseph Ryan in the film *Von Ryan's Express*, directed by Mark Robson. Sinatra played a US pilot shot down over Italy in 1943 and taken prisoner by the Germans.

'There are moments when it's too quiet. Particularly late at night or early in the mornings. That's when you know there's something lacking in your life. You just know.'

Frank Sinatra

1965 / Frank Sinatra, aged 49, poses at the entrance to his main residence, in Palm Springs, California.

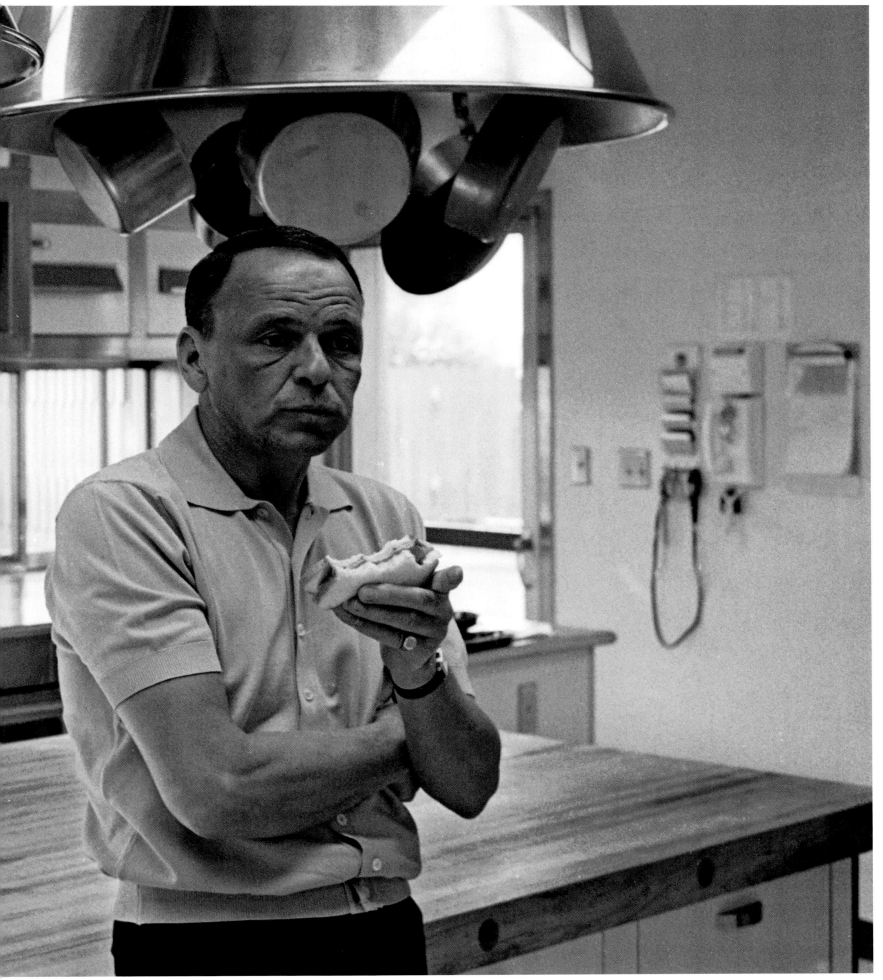

Previous pages:
1964 / Frank Sinatra permits a rare photo session in the privacy of his Californian home. He was passionate about cooking, particularly Italian cuisine, and installed a professional kitchen in his Palm Springs house.

1964 / Behind the artist, seated at the piano, is a model of one of his private jets.

1964 / Frank Sinatra at the wheel of his 1960 Ghia L 6.4. Only 26 of these exquisite cars were ever produced.

'Don't tell me. Suggest. But don't tell me.'

Frank Sinatra

1965 / Frank Sinatra and Elvis Presley performed a jazzy interpretation of 'Love Me Tender' on Sinatra's CBS television series.

1965 / Jazz singer Ella Fitzgerald sang a medley with Frank Sinatra in the NBC television studios.

1967 / Frank Sinatra and his daughter Nancy, their affection for each other obvious in these photos, came together to record the song 'Somethin' Stupid', for the album *The World We Knew*. Their collaboration was highly successful, and the song climbed to the top of the Billboard chart.

'I think my greatest ambition in life is to pass on to others what I know.'

Frank Sinatra

Previous pages
1965 / Frank Sinatra at home in Los Angeles.

116

1970 / Portrait of Frank Sinatra, aged 55.

1966 / On 19 July, Mia Farrow become Frank Sinatra's third wife. She was 21, he 50. It was a union as passionate as it was furtive; in 1968, the crooner served her with divorce papers while Farrow was on the set of *Rosemary's Baby*, under the direction of Roman Polanski.

'Fresh air makes me throw up. I can't handle it. I'd rather be around three De Nobili cigars blowing in my face all night.'

Frank Sinatra

'For him, paradise is a place with only women and, above all, no journalists.'

Humphrey Bogart

Previous pages:
1965 / Frank Sinatra appears at the Eden Roc Hotel, in Miami Beach, Florida. This establishment, which still welcomes the stars, was at the time a favourite haunt of members of the Rat Pack.

128

1967 / A last-minute shave before a shot, during the production of *Tony Rome*.

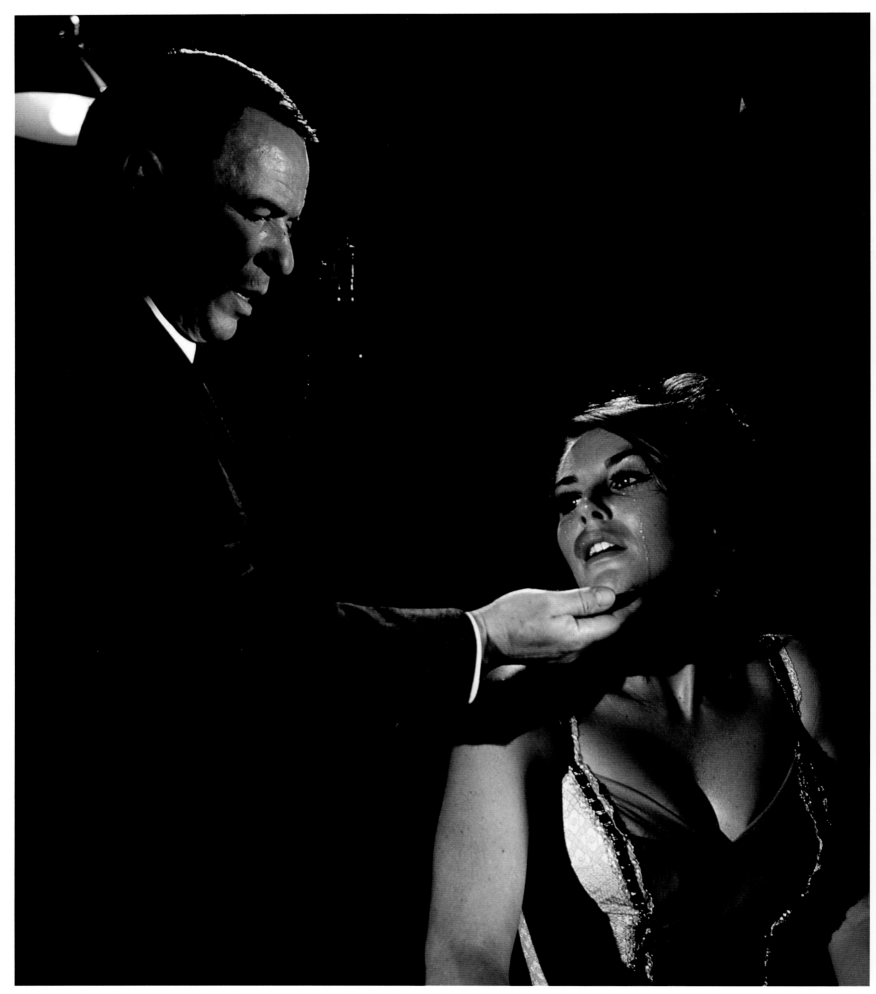

1967 / Frank Sinatra played detective Tony Rome, together with the gorgeous Jill St John, in the film adaptation of Marvin Albert's novel *Miami Mayhem*.

1967 / Shooting *Tony Rome*, which was directed by Gordon Douglas. Frank Sinatra was elegant and nonchalant in the role of a Miami private detective who is hired by a millionaire to find his daughter's stolen jewels.

1968 / Poster for the film *Lady in Cement*, directed by Gordon Douglas, in which Sinatra reprised the role of suave detective Tony Rome, which he had incarnated the year before in the eponymous film.

1968 / Frank Sinatra and American actress Raquel Welch, during the shooting of *Lady in Cement*, directed by Gordon Douglas.

'I wish that one of these days somebody would learn to do [my art] so it doesn't die where it is.'

Frank Sinatra

Previous pages:
1968 / Frank Sinatra and Raquel Welch, the two stars of *Lady In Cement*, share a relaxed moment between takes.

1961 / Portrait of Frank Sinatra, aged 45.

136

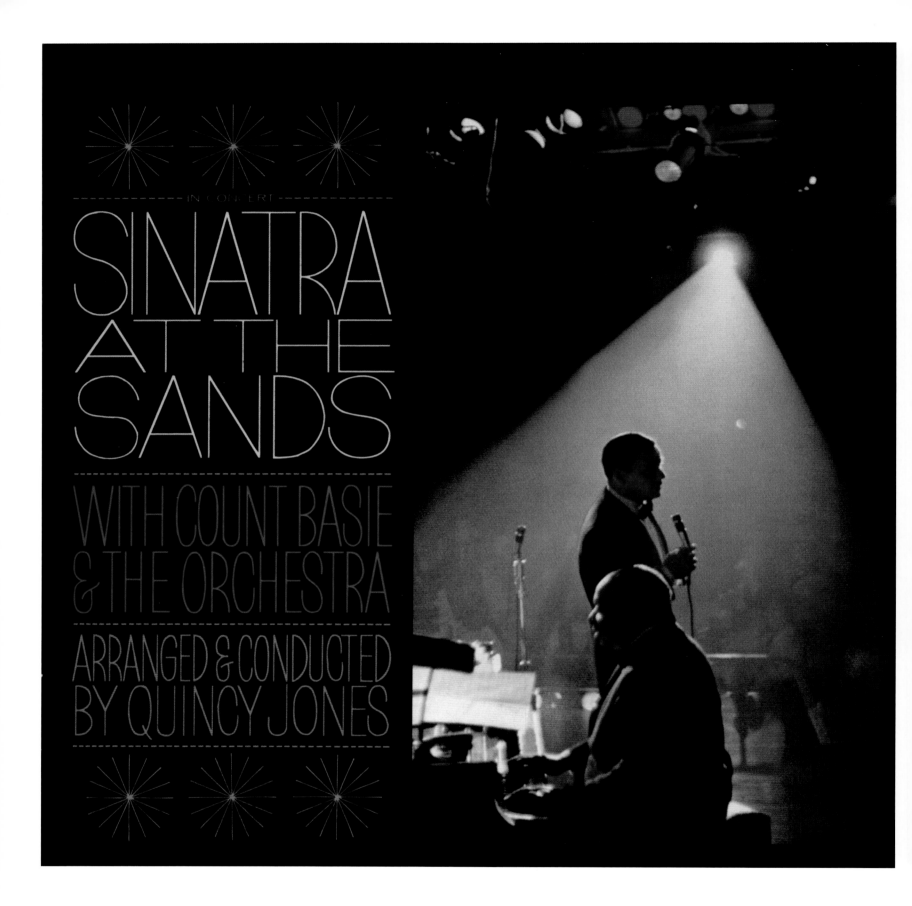

Previous pages:
1966 / Frank Sinatra and Count Basie prepare to go on stage at the Sands, in Las Vegas.

1966 / The album *Sinatra at the Sands* was recorded in the Copa Room of the Sands Hotel, in Las Vegas. It was the very first 'live' album released by the crooner.

1966 / The live recording of *Sinatra at the Sands*, with Count Basie and his Orchestra, is considered a landmark. Superbly arranged by Quincy Jones, the record showcased an inspired and nuanced Sinatra, as well as the magical rhythm and sophisticated, fluid style of pianist Count Basie.

'I hope that you live to be 100 and that the last thing you hear is my voice.'

Frank Sinatra

Previous pages:
1966 / With his perfectly fitting blue suit and bow tie, Sinatra presented a picture of charm and elegance to his audience.

144

1971 / Portrait of Frank Sinatra, aged 55, wearing his favourite colour – orange.

1965 / Frank Sinatra and his long-standing accompanist, the American jazz pianist Bill Miller. The two men collaborated in rehearsals, both on stage and on set, for more than fifty years.

1973 / Two years after first saying goodbye to the stage and the world of show business, Frank Sinatra went back into the studio to record *Ol' Blue Eyes is Back*. To mark the release of the album, he performed two landmark concerts in Los Angeles.

1975 / Photographer Terry O'Neill followed Frank Sinatra around during his preparations for a concert at the London Palladium. The theatre received more than 350,000 requests for tickets to this single concert.

1967 / Sinatra performed a sold-out concert at Madison Square Garden, in New York.

14 May 1998

Frank Sinatra dies of a heart attack in Los Angeles, at the age of 82. Over the course of his career, he made 60 films and sold more than 150 million albums. Nicknamed 'The Voice', he changed the world of music forever. More than ten years after his death, he remains the most played singer on radio; every two seconds, somewhere in the world, a radio programme plays one of his songs.

Previous pages:
1984 / From 7 to 22 September, a triumphant Frank Sinatra packed the Royal Albert Hall for six concerts, before the cream of London society. The press were unanimous in hailing him the greatest vocalist of the century.

Discography

Columbia

1946	*The Voice of Frank Sinatra*
1947	*Songs by Sinatra*
1948	*Christmas Songs by Sinatra*
1949	*Frankly Sentimental*
1950	*Dedicated to You*
1950	*Swing and Dance with Frank Sinatra*
1955	*The Voice*

Capitol

1954	*Songs for Young Lovers*
1954	*Swing Easy!*
1955	*In the Wee Small Hours*
1956	*Songs for Swingin' Lovers*
1956	*This Is Sinatra!*
1957	*Close to You and More*
1957	*A Swingin' Affair!*
1957	*Where Are You?*
1957	*A Jolly Christmas from Frank Sinatra*
1958	*Come Fly with Me*
1958	*This Is Sinatra Volume 2*
1958	*Frank Sinatra Sings for Only the Lonely*
1959	*Come Dance with Me!*
1959	*Look to Your Heart*
1959	*No One Cares*
1960	*Nice 'n' Easy*
1961	*Sinatra's Swingin' Session!!!*
1961	*All the Way*
1961	*Come Swing With Me*
1962	*Point of No Return*
1962	*Sinatra Sings of Love and Things*

Reprise

1961	*Ring-A-Ding-Ding*
196	*Swing Along With Me*
1961	*I Remember Tommy*
1962	*Sinatra and Strings*
1962	*Sinatra and Swingin' Brass*
1962	*All Alone*
1962	*Sinatra Sings Great Songs from Great Britain*
1962	*Sinatra–Basie: An Historic Musical First*
1963	*The Concert Sinatra*
1963	*Sinatra's Sinatra*
1964	*Sinatra Sings Days of Wine and Roses, Moon River, and Other Academy Award Winners*
1964	*America, I Hear You Singing*
1964	*It Might as Well Be Swing*
1964	*12 Songs of Christmas*
1964	*Softly, As I Leave You*
1965	*Sinatra '65: The Singer Today*
1965	*September of My Years*

Discography

1965	*My Kind of Broadway*
1965	*A Man and His Music*
1966	*Moonlight Sinatra*
1966	*Strangers in the Night*
1966	*Sinatra at the Sands with Count Basie*
1966	*That's Life*
1967	*Francis Albert Sinatra & Antonio Carlos Jobim*
1967	*The World We Knew*
1968	*Francis A. & Edward K.*
1968	*Frank Sinatra's Greatest Hits*
1968	*The Sinatra Family Wish You a Merry Christmas*
1968	*Cycles*
1969	*My Way*
1969	*A Man Alone*
1970	*Watertown*
1971	*Sinatra & Company*
1972	*Frank Sinatra's Greatest Hits Vol. 2*
1973	*Ol' Blue Eyes Is Back*
1974	*Some Nice Things I've Missed*
1974	*The Main Event – Live*
1980	*Trilogy: Past Present Future*
1981	*She Shot Me Down*

Qwest

1984	*L.A. Is My Lady*
	The last Capitol albums
1993	*Duets*
1994	*Duets II*
	Post-career albums with new material
1994	*Sinatra & Sextet: Live in Paris* (live)
1995	*Sinatra 80th: Live in Concert* (live)
1997	*With Red Norvo Quintet: Live in Australia, 1959* (live)
1999	*Sinatra '57 in Concert* (live)
2005	*Live from Las Vegas* (live)
2006	*Sinatra: Vegas* (live)
2009	*Live at the Meadowlands* (live)
	Albums conducted by Sinatra
1946	*Frank Sinatra Conducts The Music Of Alec Wilder*
1956	*Frank Sinatra Conducts Tone Poems of Color*
1957	*The Man I Love* (Sung by Peggy Lee, arranged by Nelson Riddle)
1958	*Sleep Warm* (Sung by Dean Martin)
1962	*Frank Sinatra Conducts Music From Pictures And Plays*
1982	*Syms by Sinatra* (Sung by Sylvia Syms)
1983	*What's New?* (with trumpeter Charles Turner)
	Rat Pack live concert albums
1993	*Frank Sinatra, Dean Martin, Sammy Davis Jr at Villa Venice, Chicago Live 1962*
1999	*Frank, Sammy & Dean: The Summit in Concert*
2001	*The Rat Pack Live at the Sands*
2002	*Ratpack: From Vegas to St. Louis*
2002	*Christmas with the Rat Pack*
2003	*The Ultimate Rat Pack Collection: Live & Swingin'*

Filmography

Filmography

1962	*The Road to Hong Kong*, directed by Norman Panama
1962	*The Manchurian Candidate*, directed by John Frankenheimer
1963	*The List of Adrian Messenger*, directed by John Huston
1963	*Come Blow Your Horn,* directed by Bud Yorkin
1963	*A New Kind of Love*, directed by Melville Shavelson
1963	*4 for Texas*, directed by Robert Aldrich
1964	*Paris – When It Sizzles*, directed by Richard Quine
1964	*Robin and the 7 Hoods*, directed by Gordon Douglas
1965	*None But the Brave*, directed by Frank Sinatra
1965	*Von Ryan's Express*, directed by Mark Robson
1965	*Marriage on the Rocks*, directed by Jack Donohue
1966	*Cast a Giant Shadow*, directed by Melville Shavelson
1966	*Assault on a Queen*, directed by Jack Donohue
1967	*The Naked Runner,* directed by Sidney J Furie
1967	*Tony Rome*, directed by Gordon Douglas
1968	*The Detective,* directed by Gordon Douglas
1968	*Lady in Cement*, directed by Gordon Douglas
1970	*Dirty Dingus Magee*, directed by Burt Kennedy
1970	'A Christmas Night with the Stars' (TV series – 1 episode)
1977	*Contract on Cherry Street,* directed by William A Graham (film for TV)
1980	*The First Deadly Sin*, directed by Brian G Hutton
1987	'Magnum, P.I.', directed by Donald P Bellisario and Glen A Larson (TV series – 1 episode)
1995	*Young at Heart*, directed by Allan Arkush (film for TV)
1996	'Hey Arnold!', directed by Craig Bartlett (TV series – 1 episode)

Director

1965	*None But the Brave,* directed by Frank Sinatra

Producer

1956	*Johnny Concho*, directed by Don McGuire
1959	*A Hole in the Head*, directed by Frank Capra
1961	*X-15*, directed by Richard Donner
1962	*Sergeants 3*, directed by John Sturges
1924	*Robin and the 7 Hoods*, directed by Gordon Douglas
1965	*None But the Brave*, directed by Frank Sinatra
1969	*Frank Sinatra: Sinatra*, directed by Tim Kiley (film for TV)
1980	*The First Deadly Sin*, directed by Brian G Hutton
1981	*All-Star Inaugural Gala*

I would like to thank Studio Gorne for their pre-press work and for their involvement in this project.

Your excellent work in the scanning and retouching of images of Frank Sinatra has given new life to rare and forgotten photographs.

Thanks for your enthusiasm and passion for images.

Acknowledgments

Fly me to the moon
Let me play among the stars
Let me see what spring is like on
Jupiter and Mars

(...) In other words, please be true
In other words, I love you

('Fly Me to the Moon' – BART HOWARD, 1954)

Mounia, this book is for you ...

My happiness is our family,
My dream that it continues to grow.
I am the happiest of men.

Yann-Brice

My thoughts go also to Alain Rish and Laurent-Paul Gros.
Wherever you are today, I hope that you too will be soothed by the warmth of Sinatra's sweet notes ...
We miss you.

Finally, I would like to thank Iannis Domon and Patricia Vincent for their valuable assistance in my photo research and their constant involvement to produce documents of the highest possible quality.

Y-B Dherbier

Credits